GW01288202

SONGS OF GOD'S PEOPLE

THE PSALMS MADE FOR SINGING

MARTIN E LECKEBUSCH

VOLUME TWO

kevin
mayhew

We hope you enjoy *Songs of God's People, Volume 2*.
Further copies are available from your local Kevin Mayhew stockist.

In case of difficulty, please contact the publisher direct by writing to:

The Sales Department
KEVIN MAYHEW LTD
Buxhall
Stowmarket
Suffolk IP14 3BW

Phone 01449 737978
Fax 01449 737834
E-mail info@kevinmayhewltd.com

Please ask for our complete catalogue of outstanding Church Music.

First published in Great Britain in 2002 by Kevin Mayhew Ltd.

© Copyright 2002 Kevin Mayhew Ltd.

ISBN 1 84003 995 7
ISMN M 57024 147 7
Catalogue No: 1450264

0 1 2 3 4 5 6 7 8 9

Cover design by Angela Selfe
Music setter: Donald Thomson
Proof reader: Linda Ottewell

Printed and bound in Great Britain

With love to

Muriel Leckebusch

who has been my mother for all of my life
and more than half of her own.

'*...grant us and all our families*
the joys of grace'

Introduction

Has there ever been a time when the psalms were *not* relevant to Christian living? It almost goes without saying that some of them are well known and well loved precisely because they have spoken to countless Christians across the centuries of the church's existence, whatever their particular circumstances and whatever their theology or tradition of worship. This has happened at least in part because the psalmists touched on what was real and vital in their own walk with God, and expressed it in ways which have remained accessible to the community of faith. But while this is obvious for the most familiar psalms, it is also true for the lesser-known parts of the psalter, as I have found in writing the texts in this book.

When the idea of producing a set of new hymns based on the psalms was first discussed, Kevin Mayhew and I agreed an initial selection which included a number of the psalms set in the various lectionaries for major festivals, plus several of those best-known 'favourites'. The result was that the predecessor to this book'[1] reflected a quarter of the psalter but included more than its fair share of the 'easy' psalms. In preparing this volume, therefore, I have been made to look more closely at some psalms with which I was less familiar.

In several cases I have been astonished to see again how relevant the psalms are. Although they come from a different time and place, they do speak to the dilemmas which confront the human race at the opening of the twenty-first century – sometimes directly, sometimes less obviously, but often powerfully. I hope that the following examples will serve to illustrate this, and also show how I have tried to remain true to the psalms while at the same time producing verses which today's and tomorrow's congregations could sing.

Refugees and persecution

The plight of refugees is a global problem. We see it frequently in the news: in the almost unbelievable numbers fleeing this war or that dictator, or in the debate about how to treat asylum seekers who arrive in 'our' country. But it is brought home to us with fresh urgency and poignancy by individuals – such as the Croatian family whose son attends the same playgroup as my daughter.

Yet the phenomenon is by no means entirely modern either: there is ample Biblical witness to similar problems. How old was Jesus when the Magi, coming to worship him, unwittingly alerted Herod the Great to his birth? How long did the family spend as refugees in Egypt? And if it is the big events which stand out among our earliest memories, could it be that Christ grew up with at least some hazy awareness of a foreign land and a long homeward journey? Persecution and migration are a significant part of our spiritual heritage.

The psalms, too, make us aware of this. The chosen people were exiled, driven from their own land by the judgement of God (which is not to say that all refugees deserve their sufferings – far from it!). Psalm 137 is a reminder of Judah's exile. Here we have hints of the issues of identity, of a clash of cultures, of ridicule for foreigners . . . As a basis for congregational song, this psalm is problematic. It seemed best to reorder the ideas it expresses, to end on a more positive and challenging note. But what are we to make of the vindictive parts of the psalm? While pondering this I remembered the Old Testament dictum, 'eye for eye, tooth for tooth.'[2] Were the exiles perhaps expressing pain at what had happened to them and their children? ('How would you like it, Babylonians?') This is the train of thought behind the second stanza of *By foreign streams we sat and wept for Zion.*

Sometimes, though, God's people have been persecuted for no other reason than their beliefs. Christians do not have a monopoly on this kind of suffering either, for numerous groups, religious, ethnic, social and so on, have faced discrimination. Nor has the church always been free of guilt in these matters. Nevertheless, suffering of this kind raises particular difficulties for people of faith: 'Why has God abandoned us?' remains a probing question. In this volume, Psalms 74 and 79 pose that question; in the former, 'remember' seemed to be a key word, while the latter records indignities suffered by the Jewish people which seem quite closely to parallel the experiences of, for example, various Bosnian communities during the Balkan conflicts of the last few years.

Anxiety and depression

To share distress within a group is one thing; to feel that one is alone in one's distress takes the anguish to new depths. The psalmists were not immune to such experiences, and many of their words carry an intensity of feeling as potent as anything we might expect from a modern poet. The nadir of bleakness is Psalm 88: 'There is no sadder prayer in the Psalter,' remarks Derek Kidner[3], adding that this psalm does not have the happy ending of most similar psalms, finishing as it does with the word *darkness.*

This psalmist was not unique in his despair – not even among those who write songs for God's people to use in worship. A striking example among hymnwriters is William Cowper (1731-1800). John White, writing from the perspective of a Christian who is also a qualified psychiatrist, comments on Cowper's hymn *O for a closer walk with God*:

> *Where is the blessedness I knew*
> *when first I saw the Lord?*
> *Where is the soul-refreshing view*
> *of Jesus and his word?*

White says, 'I notice the beginnings of his morbid disposition ... the verse might pass for spiritual ardour if we did not know better. A later hymn reveals clearer signs of pathology ...

> *I hear but seem to hear in vain*
> *insensible as steel;*
> *if aught is felt, 'tis only pain*
> *to find I cannot feel.'* [4]

Being a believer guarantees no immunity to anxiety: in fact, it may actually make things worse. Someone who has no faith may ultimately write off life's difficulties as the arbitrary products of a meaningless universe. Faith demands rather that there must be some reason, some answer and by implication some way through. Moreover, if I believe this but cannot see the way forward, I may feel guilt at my lack of joy. Can such feelings and ideas, and the psalms which reflect them, properly find a place in our worship? Are Psalms 88, 13 and the like suitable for congregational singing?

I have tried to use these psalms to create texts which *could* be used by a congregation – though, admittedly, this has meant toning down their bleakest elements. I have, however, attempted still to reflect the difficulties: *When anxious thoughts assail my mind* (Psalm 13) is an affirmation of faith amid the realities of the struggle; *Day and night I cry to you* (Psalm 88) tries to recognise the thoughts of despair and the way they may go round and round in the mind. Perhaps texts like these might contribute to worship in at least two ways: by giving someone who did feel imprisoned by despair words with which to reach out to God; and by helping other Christians to understand a little more of how such anguish feels.

Many faiths – and none

A hundred years ago, Christianity was the majority faith in perhaps every country in the Western world. No longer is that the case. The gradual erosion of belief, the rise of an increasingly secular society, the diminishing influence of church and Bible on both individual attitudes and national life – all these have gathered pace to the extent that in many lands practising Christians are now at most a substantial minority. Add to this such factors as large-scale population movements, the increasing zeal of Islam, the growth in popularity of Eastern religions such as Buddhism and the resurgence of paganism with the 'new age' movement, and it swiftly becomes apparent that Christians are certainly not the only religious community in our society. How are we to respond to this?

Here, too, the psalmists have something pertinent to say to us. A number of the psalms were also written in a 'multi-faith' setting, as prophetic voices in Israel sought to remind the people that there was only one God: the Lord, the Creator of heaven and earth and the Redeemer of the tribes of Israel. The writer of Psalm 135, for example, reminded his hearers that the Lord was greater than all the other gods their neighbours chose to revere – for he made and sustained the world. This psalm pours scorn on the ability of idols made by human hands to save their adherents. So does Psalm 115. Can we use these psalms in a pluralist society?

Maybe that is the wrong question to ask. Rather, can we truly call ourselves Christians if we fail to assert – humbly, but firmly – the uniqueness of the faith revealed through the Bible, namely, the truth of Jesus Christ, incarnate, crucified and raised from the dead? The New Testament writers certainly believed that they were building on the foundation of Old Testament monotheism, even though it rapidly became apparent that the new faith could not be contained in the old structures of Judaism. Perhaps we need to stand up and be counted again, and to reaffirm our conviction that our God, Father, Son and Holy Spirit, is the only true God, the Maker of everything, who commands all people everywhere to repent.[5]

What of men and women who profess no faith and whose lives are lived without reference to anything beyond the material world? In Psalm 53 we find a stinging rebuke for those who say there is no God: David describes them as 'morally deficient'[6]. However, before we point the finger we must note that his words are applied to everyone – and are quoted in Romans by the apostle Paul, as he exposes universal human sinfulness. I found that it was this aspect which most struck me as I wondered how to shape Psalm 53 for today: how much do I, although a Christian, live as if there were no God? The resultant text, *Who dares imagine a life spent without you?*, sits more lightly on the psalm than the majority in this book, but I feel it does have a relevance to the practical business of living as if we really believed what our creeds declare – in other words, to Christian discipleship.

Acknowledgements

Once more, I extend my thanks to Kevin Mayhew, without whose initial suggestion and continued encouragement the majority of these hymns would not have been written. Thanks are also due to the many people at Kevin Mayhew Ltd. who have played a part in bringing this book to publication.

As in the first volume of *Songs of God's People*, I must express my gratitude to the composers whose music has changed my words into songs fit for singing. It is both exciting and humbling to find such a range of musicians – and from so many different places, right round the world! – taking the time to add another dimension to my texts.

My family remain a source of strength and encouragement. Jane, my wife, continues to be patient with my preoccupation for hymns, even when it threatens to dominate everything else; my daughters make sure that it cannot fulfil that threat. But since the last texts in this volume reached their final form on my fortieth birthday, it seems timely to dedicate the collection to my mother, with thanks for her love, support and encouragement over the decades.

Most of all, the honour is the Lord's. Looking back over the writing of these texts, it is again apparent that I could not have produced them without the prompting and guidance of the Holy Spirit. In saying this I do not wish to claim that every phrase is divinely inspired, nor to deny that using God-given gifts involves a holy duty to work at developing those gifts. What I *do* want to affirm is the sense that the Lord has been with me as I have tried to open up the psalms and offer them in a fresh way to God's people as songs to sing. So my prayer remains:

> *...may we who live on earth*
> *extol you all our days,*
> *and seize each opportunity*
> *to sing your praise.*[7]

1. *Songs of God's People: The Psalms made for singing, Volume 1*, Kevin Mayhew
2. For example, Leviticus 24: 20.
3. *Psalms 73-150: A commentary on books III-V of the Psalms*, Derek Kidner, IVP, p316
4. *The Masks of Melancholy*, John White, IVP, p143. The Cowper text quoted is *The Lord will happiness divine*.
5. See Paul's sermon in Athens, Acts 17, especially v.30.
6. 'The Hebrew words rendered *fool* in Psalms denote one who is morally deficient' – footnote to Psalm 14:1, *The Holy Bible: New International Version*, Hodder & Stoughton.
7. *The honour, Lord, is yours*, stanza 4; based on Psalm 115.

When anxious thoughts assail

Psalm 13

Martin E. Leckebusch

Rosalie Bonighton

JASMINE 8 8 8 10

an - xious thoughts as - sail my mind, when I be - gin to doubt your
call to you to ans - wer soon, to turn my dark - ness in - to

care, when gloom and sor - row flood my soul, I bring my
light, for life can be a bat - tle - field — un - less you

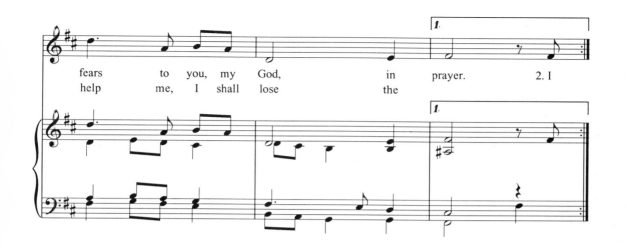

fears to you, my God, in prayer. 2. I
help me, I shall lose the

fight! 3. Yet in your end-less love I trust, in your sal-

Harmony

3. Yet in your end-less love I trust, in your sal-

-vation I re - joice: be - cause you have been good to

be - cause you have been

-vation I re - joice: be - cause you have been good to

me I of - fer you my praise with heart and voice.

good to me I of - fer you my praise with heart and voice.

me I of - fer you my praise with heart and voice.

Lord, I approach your sanctuary

Psalm 15

Martin E. Leckebusch

Andrew Fletcher

WYLDE GREEN 88 88 (LM)

1. Lord, I approach your sanctuary — but as I come to seek your face the challenges of holiness confront me in this sacred place.

2. Your searchlight falls across my path — what flaws and failures will it show? Am I content to speak the truth, to slander neither friend nor foe?

3. Esteem for those who savour sin, disdain for those who fear your name — Lord, if such attitudes are mine, then I deserve to suffer shame.

4. If I neglect some costly pledge, or let a bribe distort my sight, or simply disregard the poor — convict me, Lord, of wrong and right.

5. Give me a single-minded faith,
an eager ear for your command;
make mine a life securely built
on solid rock, not shifting sand.

For help in troubled times we pray

Psalm 20

Martin E. Leckebusch

John Jordan

EVERARD 86 86 (CM)

1. For help in trou - bled times we pray, for grace when life is hard, and for the pre - sence of our God to com - fort, guide and guard.

2. We ask the boun - ty of suc - cess on ev - 'ry right de - sire, a - that God sees all the heights to which our thoughts a - spire.

3. If hu - man skill was all we had, how swift - ly we would fall; our on - ly hope is in the Lord, who ans - wers when we call.

4. The best re - sourc - es this world gives will fail, de - cay or rust; the God of heav'n has end - less strength — him a - lone we trust.

A steadfast heart

Psalm 26

Martin E. Leckebusch

Alan Viner

DAPHNE 88 86

Last time

2. To shun de -
3. Be clean my
4. The schemes of
5. A stead - fast

- ly.

Last time

5. A steadfast heart, a blameless life:
   may this be your work, Lord, in me,
   until I sing, with all the saints,
   your praise eternally.

I call to you, my Rock

Psalm 28

Martin E. Leckebusch

Michael Higgins

EARLSDON 66 66 88

The thrill of God's forgiveness

Psalm 32

Martin E. Leckebusch

Andrew Wright

HADLEY 76 76 D

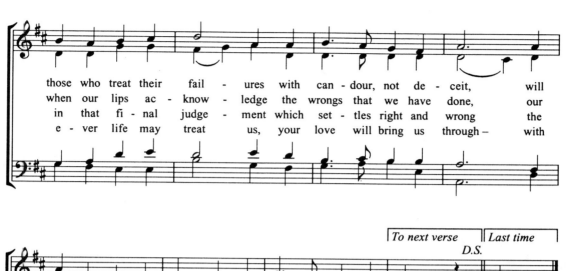

those who treat their fail - ures with can - dour, not de - ceit, will
when our lips ac - know - ledge the wrongs that we have done, our
in that fi - nal judge - ment which set - tles right and wrong the
e - ver life may treat us, your love will bring us through – with

To next verse | Last time
D.S.

find in God's ac - cep - tance their joy is made com - plete.
peace is re - in - sta - ted, our guil - ty load is gone.
Lord will be our re - fuge, his sav - ing pow'r, our song.
all who know your mer - cy we will re - joice in you.

To next verse | Last time
D.S.

Be joyful, be skilful

Psalm 33

Martin E. Leckebusch

Rosalie Bonighton

RAINFOREST 11 11

1. Be joy-ful, be skil-ful, and come with new songs— give
3. vere him whose word set the o - ceans in place, whose
5. heart he ex - a - mines, our se - crets are known; how

praise to the Lord, for to him it be - longs! 2. In
voice sent the stars on their jour - neys through space. 4. Through
hap - py we are — still he makes us his own! 6. Though

all things the Lord is proved faith - ful and right, for
all ge - ne - ra - tions his pur - pose will stand — his
earth - ly re - sour - ces are pow'r - less to save, trust

To vs. 3 to 5

jus - tice and ho - li - ness are his de - light. 3. Re -
will o - ver - rules what the na - tions have planned. 5. Each
him, and no long - er need you fear the

Unison

grave. 7. In you, Lord, we hope, and on you we de-

Last time

Ped.

may love rest up - on us — your love with - out end.

Harmony

pend: may love rest up - on us — your love with - out end.

Out of life's quagmire I was rescued   Psalm 40

Martin E. Leckebusch

Timothy Blinko

HATFIELD 98 98 D

ans - wered my pray'r,   o - thers will hon - our you as
struc - tions?   Your will, my God, is my de -
num - ber;   my days are sel - dom free of

well.   Bles - sed are those who choose to trust
sire!   You see my wil - ling - ness to wit -
strife: come quick - ly, Lord – my foes pur - sue

you,   leav - ing all o - ther gods be - hind;
- ness –   how could I hide your word a - way?
me;   show them how sin will bring them shame.

23

un - num - bered mi - ra - cles of
Love must be cen - tral to my
You are my Res - cu - er and

mer - cy such folk are pri - vi - leged to find.
life - style, truth at the heart of all I say.
Help - er — with all your saints I praise your name.

Teach me, Lord, your compassion

Psalm 41

Martin E. Leckebusch

Norman Warren

MILLIE 76 86 D

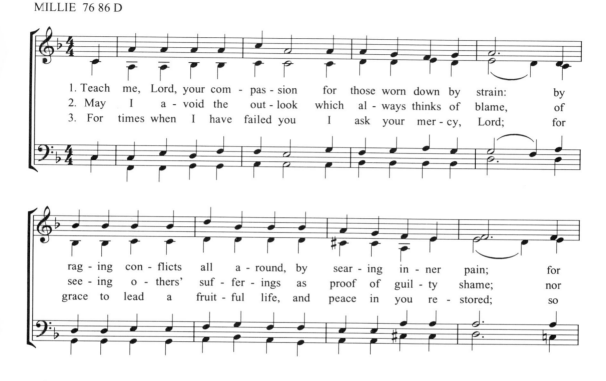

1. Teach me, Lord, your com-pas-sion for those worn down by strain: by
2. May I a-void the out-look which al-ways thinks of blame, of
3. For times when I have failed you I ask your mer-cy, Lord; for

rag-ing con-flicts all a-round, by sear-ing in-ner pain; for
see-ing o-thers' suf-fer-ings as proof of guil-ty shame; nor
grace to lead a fruit-ful life, and peace in you re-stored; so

I will need your com-fort when trou-ble reach-es me — when
let me be the rea-son for friend-ships torn in two — no
let me walk be-fore you in full in-te-gri-ty, to

pres-sure and ill-health ex-pose how fra-gile life can be.
slan-der spread, no trust a-bused, in what I say and do.
wor-ship you through-out my days and all e-ter-ni-ty.

For the honour of our King

Psalm 45

Martin E. Leckebusch

Timothy Blinko

ST ALBAN 77 76

1. For the hon - our of our King,
2. When he speaks, the truth is heard,
3. Right - eous - ness and joy are found,
4. See the splen - dour of the bride

ev - 'ry skill we have, we bring: no one
grace and pow'r in ev - 'ry word: false - hood
last - ing jus - tice will a - bound,   all be -
led in hon - our to his side: cho - sen,

stirs the heart to sing like our roy - al Mas - ter,
trem - bles at the sword of our roy - al Mas - ter,
cause the King is crowned as our roy - al Mas - ter,
loved and beau - ti - fied by her roy - al Mas - ter,

like our roy - al Mas - ter.
of our roy - al Mas - ter.
as our roy - al Mas - ter.
by her roy - al Mas - ter.

Optional Descant

5. Now, and to e - ter - nal days,

Unison

5. Now, and to e - ter - nal days, all God's

The mighty God addresses all creation Psalm 50

Martin E. Leckebusch

Rosalie Bonighton

EUCALYPTUS 11 10 11 10 11 10

1. The migh - ty God ad - dres - ses all cre - a - tion:
2. He has no need of sa - cri - fi - cial rit - uals—
3. Yet who would dare bring emp - ty words of hom - age

in storm and flame he speaks from hea - ven's throne.
of la - vish gifts, or off - 'rings made by fire;
and dis - re - gard the chal - lenge to o - bey?

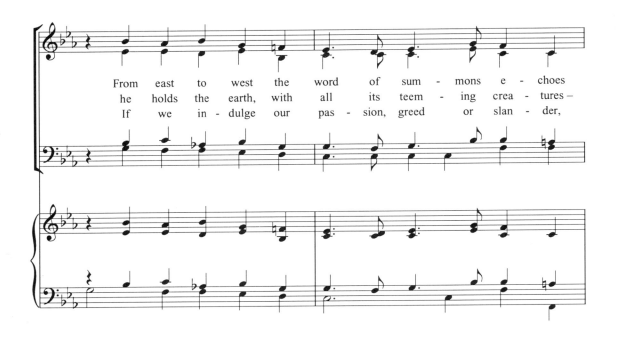

From east to west the word of sum - mons e - choes
he holds the earth, with all its teem - ing crea - tures –
If we in - dulge our pas - sion, greed or slan - der,

to ga - ther those he called to be his own;
each one is his; what more could he re - quire?
does he not grieve to see us go a - stray?

and though his right - eous - ness per - vades the cos - mos,
But thank - ful hearts, and vows which are re - mem - bered,
With thank - ful hearts, and o - pen to your voice, Lord,

the Judge him - self now makes his judge - ments known.
and hum - ble pray'rs ful - fil the Lord's de - sire.
we come to seek your new and liv - ing way.

I flourish in your presence, Lord

Psalm 52

Martin E. Leckebusch

Simon Lesley

STEYNING 86 86 88

with your saints I ce - le - brate your mer - cies old and
in their sharp and shame - ful talk de - ceit - ful plans are
pro - fit is e - ter - nal shame, both life and rich - es

new:
heard, your love sur - rounds me all my days: for -
lost?

To vs. 2 & 3

e - ver I will sing your praise.

2. Though
3. Should

To vs. 2 & 3

34

new: your love sur - rounds me   all my days: for -

new:

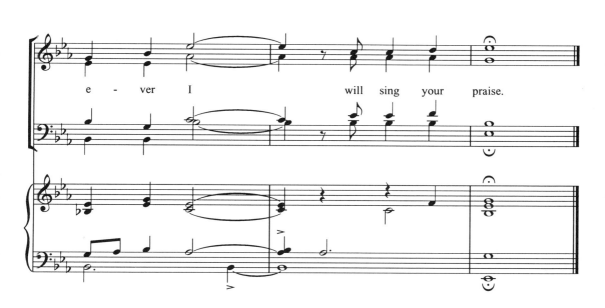

e – ver I   will sing your   praise.

Who dares imagine

Psalm 53

Martin E. Leckebusch

Betty Roe

1. Who dares im-ag-ine a life spent with-out you?
2. All of us some-times pre-tend you are ab-sent,
3. Then in our mo-ments of cri-sis we floun-der,
4. Yes, you a-lone are our wis-dom, our com-fort;

How would we know what was wrong, what was right?
liv-ing as if life were mere-ly our own,
torn by the choice bet-ween pa-nic and prayer,
on-ly in you can our joy be re-stored.

How could we han - dle our ques - tions of cons - cience,
slow to dis - co - ver the wis - dom you of - fer,
till, in our grate - ful re - lief, we ac - know - ledge:
Yes, we ad - mit it – we need you to help us,

mm,

mm,

oo,

oo,

scorn - ing your pre - sence and spurn - ing the light?
lured by the sin that we ought to dis - own.
yes, you pro - tect us – for yes, you are there!
God e - ver pre - sent, our Sa - viour, our Lord.

mm,

mm.

oo,

oo.

Last time

Oo.

Oo,

Lord, listen to my cry

Psalm 61

Martin E. Leckebusch

Robert Jones

GROSMONT 66 86 (SM)

Unison

1. Lord, lis - ten to my cry, this faint yet ur - gent plea, and guide me home - ward to a place of real se - cu - ri - ty. 2. My

Re - fuge and my Tow'r from foes on ev - 'ry side, the shel - ter you a - lone can give is where I long to hide. 3. You

know that all my vows were made for you to hear; the he - ri - tage you gave to me is built on god - ly fear. 4. Pro -

tect your ser - vant's life with - in your time - less care, and may your per - fect love be - come the crown and shield I bear. 5. For days.

To vs. 2 to 5   *Last time*

5. For then my heart's delight
   shall be to sing your praise:
   my pledge to honour you will be
   my focus all my days.

© Copyright 2002 Kevin Mayhew Ltd.

39

God my Refuge and my Rest

Psalm 62

Martin E. Leckebusch

Richard Lloyd

FONTENAY 77 77

1. God my Re-fuge and my Rest,
Men 3. Frail in-deed is hu-man strength,
5. Be my Re-fuge and my Rest;

God my Fort-ress, firm and sure,
yield - ing scant se - cu - ri - ty;
be my Fort-ress, firm and sure;

God my Sa - viour and my
brief in - deed are earth - ly
be my Sa - viour and my

Hope, in your strength I stand se - cure.
lives, mea-sured by e - ter - ni - ty.
Hope, God in whom I stand se - cure.

To vs. 2 & 4

Last time

Harmony

2. When — my foes de - vise their schemes,
4. Though my rich - es mul - ti - ply,

2. When my foes de - vise their schemes,
4. Though my rich - es mul - ti - ply,

when they mouth their cun - ning lies,
I will trust in you, my Lord:

when they mouth their cun - ning lies, you dis - cern their true in -
I will trust in you, my Lord: may my heart be yours a -

tent — who can take you by sur - prise?
lone, and your fa - vour, my re - ward.

Man.

Listen, Lord, to my complaint

Psalm 64

Martin E. Leckebusch

Norman Warren

ZACHARY 77 77

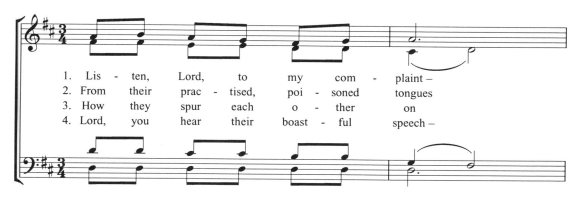

1. Lis - ten, Lord, to my com - plaint —
2. From their prac - tised, poi - soned tongues
3. How they spur each o - ther on
4. Lord, you hear their boast - ful speech —

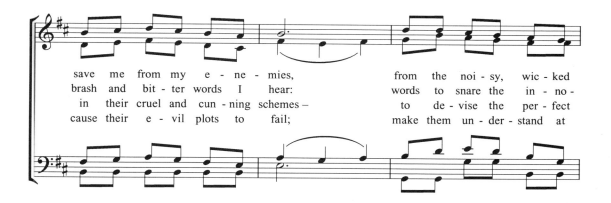

save me from my e - ne - mies,   from the noi - sy, wic - ked
brash and bit - ter words I hear: words to snare the in - no -
in their cruel and cun - ning schemes —   to de - vise the per - fect
cause their e - vil plots to fail;   make them un - der - stand at

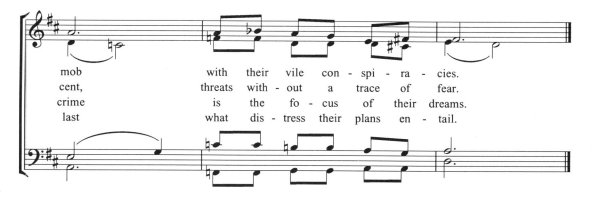

mob   with their vile con - spi - ra - cies.
cent,   threats with - out a trace of fear.
crime   is the fo - cus of their dreams.
last   what dis - tress their plans en - tail.

5. Then shall people far and near
pause and contemplate your ways –
then your servants will rejoice,
trust in you and sing your praise.

Let all the earth bring joyful songs

Psalm 66

Martin E. Leckebusch

Colin Mawby

TRIBE ROAD 10 4 10 4

1. Let all the earth bring joy - ful
   sea a - part for
   times the Lord has
   whom the faith - ful -

songs to God to praise his name, whose awe - in - spir - ing deeds and
Is - rael's sake, and led them free — for yes, the Lord sees ev - 'ry
held us safe and made us strong; let all whose lives have pros - pered
ness of God has been re - vealed: may heart - felt wor - ship be the

match - less pow'r ex - tend his fame. 2. He drove the
hu - man trial and tra - ge - dy. 3. Through trou - bled
in his love take up the song. 4. And those to
sac - ri - fice they choose to yield. 5. For by the

care.

5. For by the inmost longings of our hearts
   God weighs our prayer –
   so let us sing with reverent gratitude
   for all his care.

May God be gracious

Psalm 67

Martin E. Leckebusch

John Marsh

WELBOURN 11 10 11 10

1. May God be gra - cious, grant - ing us his
2. May all the peo - ples lift their hearts in
3. Then shall the earth re - joice in God's a -

fa - vour, shi - ning on us the kind - ness of his face,
wor - ship; may ev - 'ry na - tion bring its joy - ful song;
bun - dance – more than e - nough for ev - 'ry na - tion's need!

so that his sov - 'reign pur - pose of sal - va - tion
may they ex - alt the God who guides and jud - ges,
When all the peo - ples hon - our his in - ten - tions,

may stand re - vealed to all the hu - man race.
up - hold - ing right and o - ver - turn - ing wrong.
then shall we know God's gra - cious touch in - deed.

God, my ever-present refuge

Psalm 71

Martin E. Leckebusch

Colin Mawby

MILAN 87 87 D

Organ Introduction

1.God, my e - ver - pre - sent
earth - ly years are
God, the God of

ref - uge from the harm my foes in - tend, hear my
pas - sing, though my life may soon be gone, let to -
won - ders, who can be com - pared to you? Though I

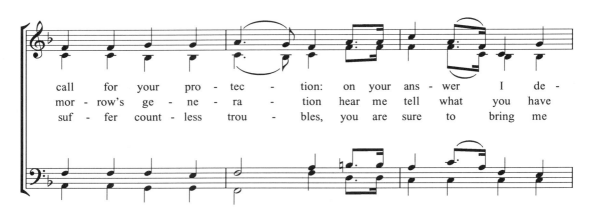

call for your pro - tec - tion: on your ans - wer I de -
mor - row's ge - ne - ra - tion hear me tell what you have
suf - fer count - less trou - bles, you are sure to bring me

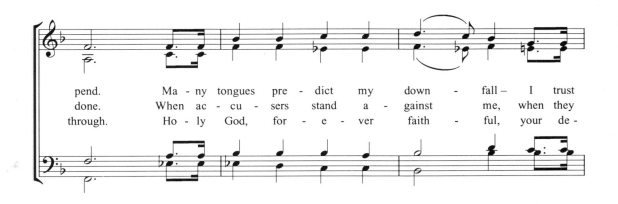

pend.   Ma - ny tongues pre - dict my down - fall — I trust
done.   When ac - cu - sers stand a - gainst me, when they
through.   Ho - ly God, for - e - ver faith - ful, your de -

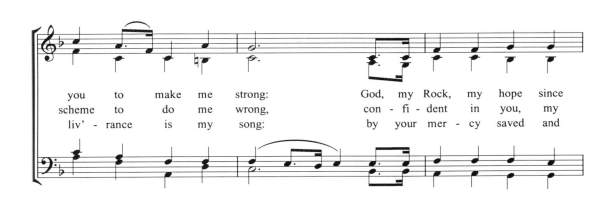

you to make me strong: God, my Rock, my hope since
scheme to do me wrong,   con - fi - dent in you, my
liv' - rance is my song: by your mer - cy saved and

To vs. 2 & 3   *Last time*

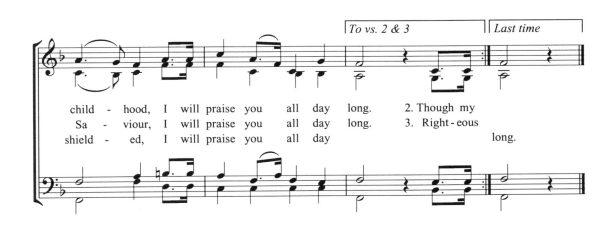

child - hood, I will praise you all day long.   2. Though my
Sa - viour, I will praise you all day long.   3. Right - eous
shield - ed, I will praise you all day   long.

Lord God, have you rejected us

Psalm 74

Martin E. Leckebusch

Andrew Moore

MEMORARE 88 88 (LM)

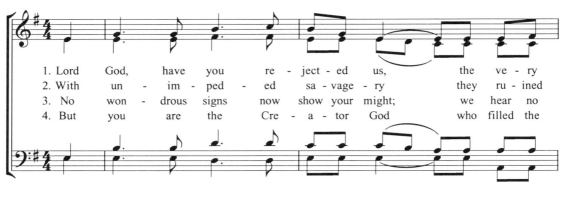

1. Lord God, have you re-ject-ed us, the ve-ry
2. With un-im-ped-ed sa-vage-ry they ru-ined
3. No won-drous signs now show your might; we hear no
4. But you are the Cre-a-tor God who filled the

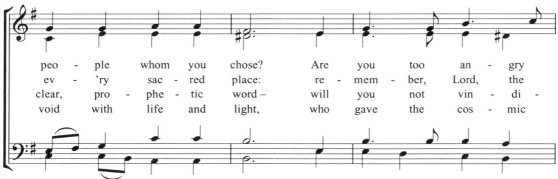

peo-ple whom you chose? Are you too an-gry
ev-'ry sac-red place: re-mem-ber, Lord, the
clear, pro-phe-tic word— will you not vin-di-
void with life and light, who gave the cos-mic

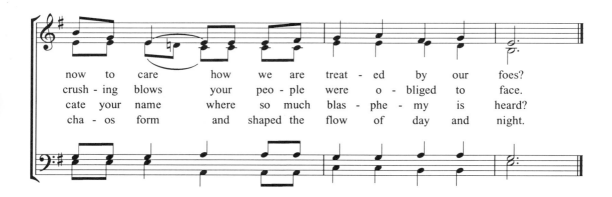

now to care how we are treat-ed by our foes?
crush-ing blows your peo-ple were o-bliged to face.
cate your name where so much blas-phe-my is heard?
cha-os form and shaped the flow of day and night.

5. Remember, Lord, your promises;
remember, Lord, your people's pain;
remember, Lord, your foes' contempt –
and reassert your holy reign!

Great God whose presence

Psalm 75

Martin E. Leckebusch

Andrew Fletcher

MARKET STREET 86 86 (CM)

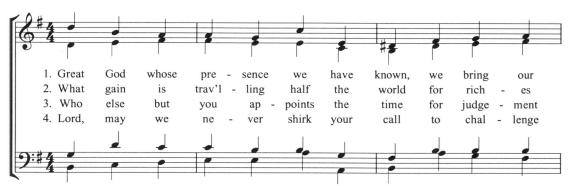

1. Great God whose pre - sence we have known, we bring our
2. What gain is trav'l - ling half the world for rich - es
3. Who else but you ap - points the time for judge - ment
4. Lord, may we ne - ver shirk your call to chal - lenge

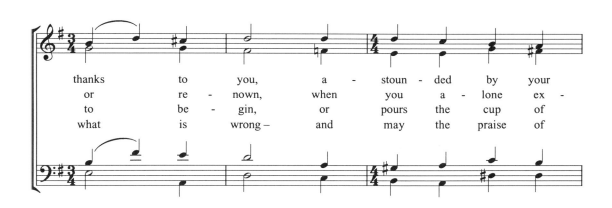

thanks to you, a - stoun - ded by your
or re - nown, when you a - lone ex -
to be - gin, or pours the cup of
what is wrong — and may the praise of

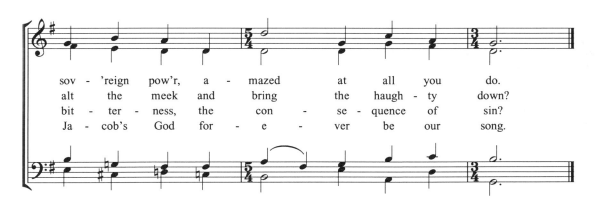

sov - 'reign pow'r, a - mazed at all you do.
alt the meek and bring the haugh - ty down?
bit - ter - ness, the con - se - quence of sin?
Ja - cob's God for - e - ver be our song.

Lord, hear your people's cry

Psalm 79

Martin E. Leckebusch

June Nixon

LEAGHUR 66 86 D (DSM)

1. Lord, hear your peo-ple's cry: what hard-ships they have
2. How long, Lord, will it be un-til you hear our
3. Re-new your peo-ple's strength and spare them fur-ther

faced! The faith-ful suf-fer ri-di-cule, their
prayer? Let those de-prived of hope and home be
shame; Lord, make your ho-ly pre-sence known and

ci-ties are laid waste; de-nied the dig-ni-
con-scious of your care; and all whose bru-tal
vin-di-cate your name! Let ev-'ry na-tion

ty   of bu - ry - ing their dead,   your
schemes   pro - voke such bit - ter pain –   how
see   the jus - tice of your ways,   till

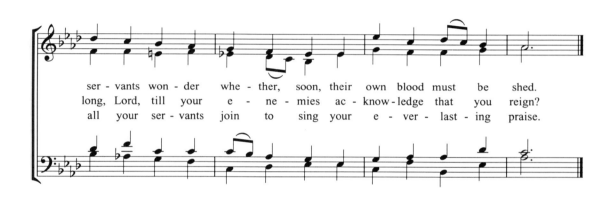

ser - vants won - der whe - ther, soon, their own blood must be shed.
long, Lord, till your e - ne - mies ac - know - ledge that you reign?
all your ser - vants join to sing your e - ver - last - ing praise.

Day and night I cry to you

Psalm 88

Martin E. Leckebusch

Martin Setchell

DIURNUS NOCTU 77 77 77

1. Day and night I cry to you: free me from my gnaw-ing fear; I am anx-ious, drained of strength, marked as one whose death is near – would I praise you from the grave? Show me, Lord, your pow'r to save.

2. How the bur-den of your wrath leaves my soul in deep dis-may! Why, so of-ten through the years, have you turned your face a-way? As a pris-'ner of des-pair, am I ban-ished from your care?

3. E-ven those I called my friends now con-si-der me un-known; dri-ven from my fa-mi-ly, I must bear my grief a-lone. In the dark-ness, ask-ing, 'Why?' night and day to you I cry.

Love will be our song for ever

Psalm 89

Martin E. Leckebusch

Michael Higgins

NEWCOMBE 87 87 D

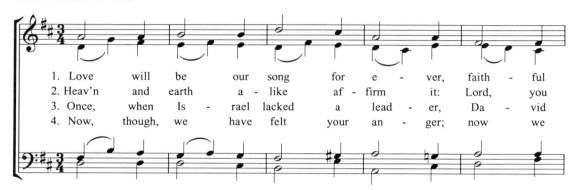

1. Love will be our song for e - ver, faith - ful
2. Heav'n and earth a - like af - firm it: Lord, you
3. Once, when Is - rael lacked a lead - er, Da - vid
4. Now, though, we have felt your an - ger; now we

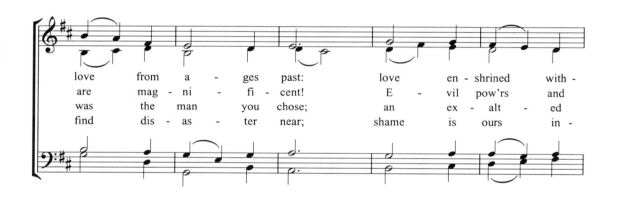

love from a - ges past: love en - shrined with -
are mag - ni - fi - cent! E - vil pow'rs and
was the man you chose; an ex - alt - ed
find dis - as - ter near; shame is ours in -

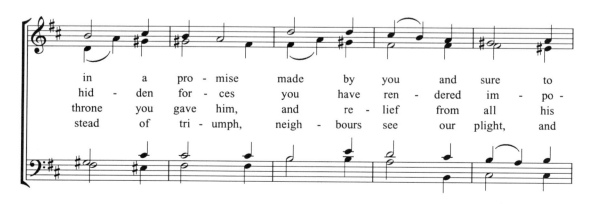

in a pro - mise made by you and sure to
hid - den for - ces you have ren - dered im - po -
throne you gave him, and re - lief from all his
stead of tri - umph, neigh - bours see our plight, and

last;   hu - man   tongues   and   an - gel
tent.   At   your   throne   of   love   and
foes;   e - ven   when   your   re - bel
sneer.   How   much   lon - ger   till   you

voi - ces   join   in   rev - 'rence   and   de -
jus - tice   we   ex - tol   you,   faith - ful
peo - ple   scorned   your   ways   and   spurned   your
hear   us?   Life   is   short,   so   swift   our

light,   prais - ing   your   un - ri - valled
King: bless'd   are   those   who   learn   to
law,   still   your   pro - mise   shaped   the
days!   Lord,   re - new   the   love   you

splen - dour,   lov - ing   Lord,   the   God   of   might.
trust   you –   they   have   am - ple   cause   to   sing.
fu - ture: love   en - dur - ing   e - ver - more.
pro - mised –   fill   your   peo - ple's   hearts   with   praise.

Let every nation bow

Psalm 99

Martin E. Leckebusch

Andrew Moore

NOMEN DOMINI 10 10 10 4

1. Let ev - 'ry na - tion bow in god - ly
2. Sing out his praise, this King of end - less
3. He gave the sac - red law which Mo - ses
4. This is our God, who hears and ans - wers

fear be - fore the Lord whom an - gels all re -
might who shows his peo - ple what is just and
taught; to him were Aa - ron's sac - ri - fi - ces
prayer, who loathes our sin, but clears the guilt we

vere; lift God's name high for all the world to
right, for right - eous - ness and truth are his de -
brought; this is the God whose fa - vour Sam - uel
bear; be - fore his throne, let heav'n and earth de -

hear —
light —
sought — ho - ly is he!
clare:

Your love will be my song

Psalm 101

Martin E. Leckebusch

Alan Viner

HAUGHMOND 66 6 D

1. Your love will be my song – Lord, keep me far from wrong, and draw me close to you: let all that you ab-hor be ban-ished e - ver - more from what I say and do.

2. The sland'-rer's dead-ly flame, and schemes that me - rit shame – in these I want no part. From ar - ro-gance and lies, from pride that clouds the eyes, my God, pro - tect my heart.

3. If a - ny-one should try to make me live a lie, con - sign their plan to fail; but glad - ly will I learn from all who can dis-cern what your com - mands en - tail.

4. Lord, I re-solve to - day in all I do and say to stand for what is true: your love will be my song, so keep me far from wrong and let me walk with you.

Sing out, my soul

Psalm 103

Martin E. Leckebusch

Richard Lloyd

CLUNY 888 67 10 77

joy God's vast ge - ne - ro - si - ty; sing, sing of un - fail - ing love, the
flow'r, so ea - si - ly swept a - way; long, long will his love re - main, sur -
praise be heard, and his pow'r dis - played! Join, join in the song, my soul, with

To verse 4 | *Last time*

crown of all who
round - ing those who fear him. 4. A -
all whose hearts re - vere him!

Man. Ped.

To verse 2 | **Harmony**

fear him. 2. With jus - tice for the

To verse 2

Man.

61

victimised the Lord has made compassion known – with mercy he rescinds the guilt of those he calls his own. High, high as the heav'ns above is the reach of God's never-ending love; far, far are their sins removed from those who truly fear him.

D.S.

Men: 3. He

D.S.

Man.

Ped.

Sing to the Lord with gratitude

Psalm 105

Martin E. Leckebusch

John Jordan

CROSSWAYS 11 10 11 10 11 10 11 12

1. Sing to the Lord with gra - ti - tude and won - der;
2. A - cross the years, a - cross the miles they jour - neyed,
3. So Is - rael made their home a - while in E - gypt;
4. They left cap - ti - vi - ty with am - ple plun - der,

in song and sto - ry tell what he has done:
both led and shield - ed by God's lov - ing hand,
they grew in num - bers and pro - spe - ri - ty
and through an emp - ty de - sert they were led;

let all the na - tions be in - spired to seek him,
un - til the scourge of fa - mine struck the na - tions,
till Pha - raoh's peo - ple dread - ed sub - ju - ga - tion
be - neath a fie - ry cloud they were pro - tect - ed,

the Migh - ty God, the Lord, the Right - eous One.
and brought des - truc - tion to that pro - mised land.
and changed their wel - come in - to sla - ve - ry.
and with the bread of an - gels they were fed.

His pro - mise came to A - bra - ham and Is - aac,
But e - ven then he marked the path be - fore them
Through Mo - ses, God con - front - ed this in - jus - tice,
Sing praise to God, whose pro - mise ne - ver fal - ters,

a land in which their fa - mi - ly could live;
when Jo - seph en - tered E - gypt as a slave –
sent plagues of judge - ment time and time a - gain,
who thrills the hearts of those he makes his friends;

his pledge en - dures a thou - sand ge - ne - ra - tions,
a man who rose to pro - mi - nence and pow - er,
then by one fi - nal blow to E - gypt's first - born
who so en - rich - es all he brings to free - dom

a co - ve - nant whose rich - es he de - lights to give.
dis - tin - guished by the god - ly coun - sel which he gave.
he set his peo - ple free and broke their ev - 'ry chain.
that they may learn to live their days as he in - tends.

Lord, I am determined

Psalm 108

Martin E. Leckebusch

Robert Jones

WELSH NEWTON 11 11 11 11

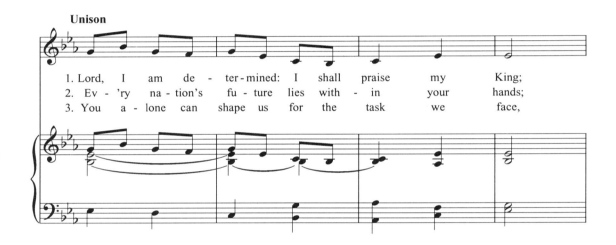

Unison

1. Lord, I am de-ter-mined: I shall praise my King;
2. Ev-'ry na-tion's fu-ture lies with-in your hands;
3. You a-lone can shape us for the task we face,

ear-ly in the mor-ning I shall rise and sing;
su-per-pow'rs are sub-ject to di-vine com-mands!
o-ver-com-ing e-vil by the pow'r of grace;

praise will be my prac - tice ev - 'ry - where I go,
In your care the cos - mos finds its des - ti - ny –
hear the cry for mer - cy ris - ing to your throne:

ne - ver hold - ing back what all the world should know.
Lord, how o - ver - whelm - ing is your ma - jes - ty!
lead us, help us, save us – make your pre - sence known!

The honour, Lord, is yours

Psalm 115

Martin E. Leckebusch

Martin Setchell

HONOUR 66 84 D

1. The honour, Lord is yours: to you all praise be giv'n, great God of love and faithfulness, enthroned in heav'n. Though many, far and
2. Unseen, yet seeing all, you hear and act and feel, unlike the shallow fantasies which some think real — those idols lack the
3. To all who search for joy, the pathway is the same: a call to serve you day by day and bear your name. Our ever-faithful
4. May you, the God of heav'n who set the stars in space, grant us and all our families the joys of grace; may we who live on

wide,   are un - a - ware of you,   your
pow'r   to think or move or speak;   the
Lord,   our Help - er and our Shield,   the
earth   ex - tol you all our days,   and

sov - 'reign will is e - vi - dent in all you do.
aid of such un - wor - thy gods we will not seek.
dreams and fears that shape our lives to you we yield.
seize each op - por - tu - ni - ty to sing your praise.

Come, praise the Lord

Psalm 117

Martin E. Leckebusch

June Nixon

TARNAGULLA 8 11 9 33 7

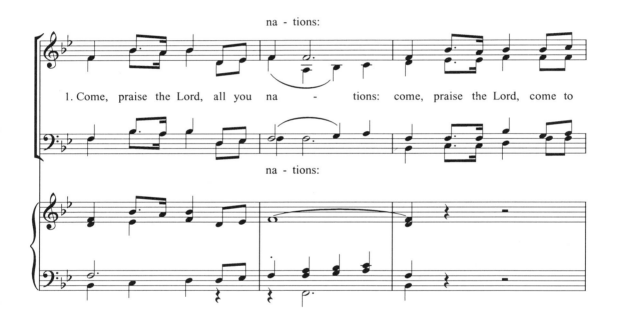

praised, to be praised, to be praised for e - ver - more.

2. Come, meet the Lord, all you

Man.

Ped.

peo - ples: come and re - joice, for his love for you is great and his
love is great

peo - ples: love for you is great

Man.

faith - ful - ness is un - end - ing — bless the Lord, bless the Lord, bless the

Lord, and ce - le - brate.

Unless the Lord had stood with us   Psalm 124

Martin E. Leckebusch

Alan Rees OSB

NISI DOMINUS 86 86 (CM)

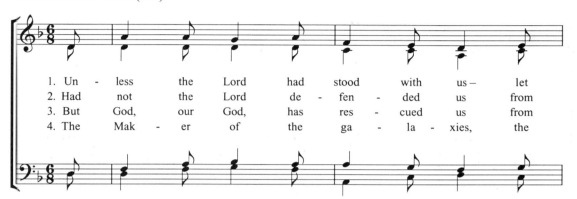

1. Un - less the Lord had stood with us – let
2. Had not the Lord de - fen - ded us from
3. But God, our God, has res - cued us from
4. The Mak - er of the ga - la - xies, the

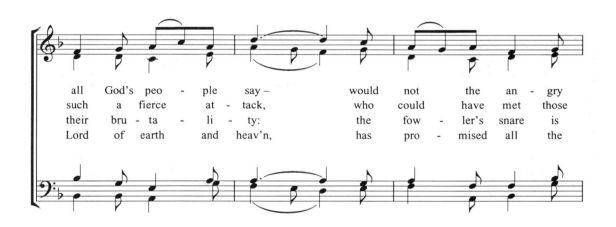

all God's peo - ple say – would not the an - gry
such a fierce at - tack, who could have met those
their bru - ta - li - ty: the fow - ler's snare is
Lord of earth and heav'n, has pro - mised all the

storms we faced have swept our lives a - way?
dread - ful foes and held the on - slaught back?
bro - ken now, the cap - tive birds fly free.
help we need – all praise to God be giv'n!

So firm and sure, those ancient hills

Psalm 125

Martin E. Leckebusch

Simon Lesley

CHACTONBURY DOWN 88 88 88

1. So firm and sure, those an - cient hills which stand a -
God of ho - li - ness, re - strains the
all whose hearts are pure, who choose to

round Je - ru - sa - lem; thus all whose faith is in the Lord will know his
ru - lers of the lands, to stay the lure of e - vil deeds from snar - ing
serve you faith - ful - ly, but un - der - mine the crook - ed schemes of those who

pow'r en - fold - ing them: these are the saints he makes se - cure,
god - ly hearts and hands: cor - rupt re - gimes will not re - main
fos - ter trea - che - ry: cause ty - ran - nies and threats to cease,

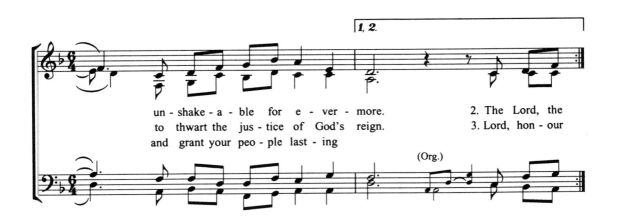

un - shake - a - ble for e - ver - more.　　2. The Lord, the
to thwart the jus - tice of God's reign.　　3. Lord, hon - our
and grant your peo - ple last - ing

(Org.)

peace.　　　A - - men.

How good it is to share

Psalm 133

Martin E. Leckebusch

Alan Rees OSB

QUAM BONUM 66 66

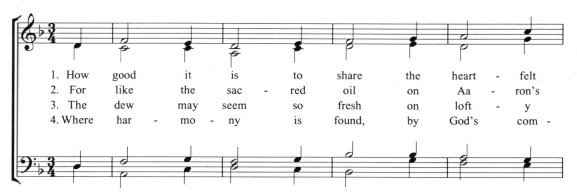

1. How good it is to share the heart - felt
2. For like the sac - red oil on Aa - ron's
3. The dew may seem so fresh on loft - y
4. Where har - mo - ny is found, by God's com -

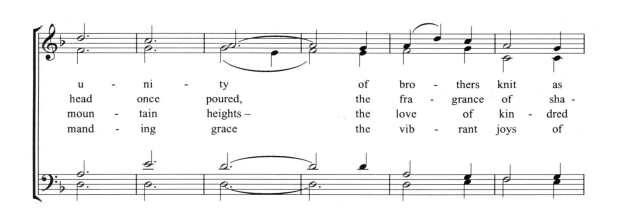

u - ni - ty of bro - thers knit as
head once poured, the fra - grance of sha -
moun - tain heights – the love of kin - dred
mand - ing grace the vib - rant joys of

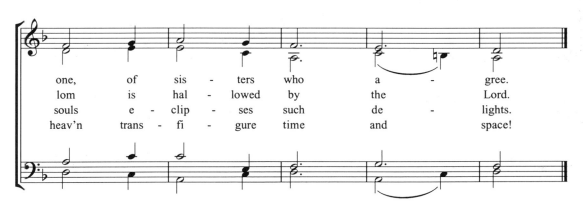

one, of sis - ters who a - gree.
lom is hal - lowed by the Lord.
souls e - clip - ses such de - lights.
heav'n trans - fi - gure time and space!

Come into God's presence

Psalm 135

Martin E. Leckebusch

John Marsh

PRIESTLY DEVOTION 11 11 11 11

1. Come in-to God's pre-sence to wor-ship and sing, with
2. The depths of the o-ceans, the stars far a-way— the
3. When E-gypt af-flic-ted the peo-ple he chose, God
4. The fame of the Lord will ex-tend e-ver-more— how

glad hal-le-lu-jahs the off-'rings you bring; how
whole of cre-a-tion falls un-der his sway; in
dealt the op-pres-sor the fierc-est of blows; and
un-like the i-dols some peo-ple a-dore! De-

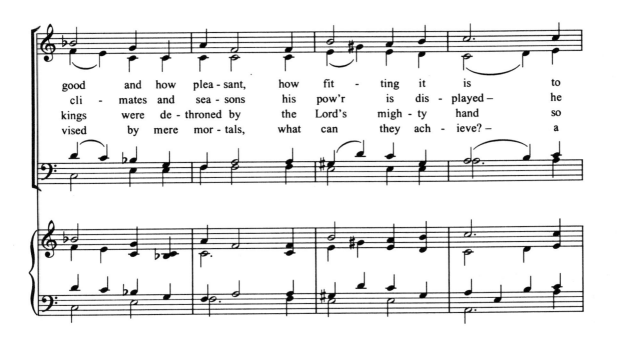

good and how plea - sant, how fit - ting it is to
cli - mates and sea - sons his pow'r is dis - played – he
kings were de - throned by the Lord's migh - ty hand so
vised by mere mor - tals, what can they ach - ieve? – a

hon - our the Lord who af - firms we are his.
does as he plea - ses with all that he made.
Is - rael could en - ter their long - pro - mised land.
fac - tor which ma - ny de - cline to per - ceive.

5. God's call made you holy, to walk in his sight
   in rev'rent submission and thankful delight –
   so come, all God's people, with off'rings of praise:
   make priestly devotion the crown of your days.

By foreign streams we sat and wept

Psalm 137

Martin E. Leckebusch

Betty Roe

WYLD 11 10 11 10

1. By for-eign streams we
2. Lord, from the pain of

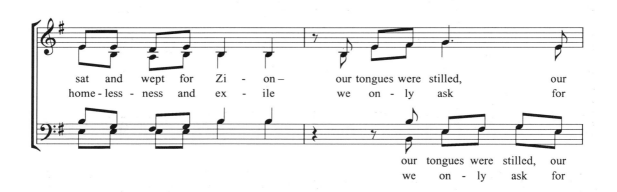

sat and wept for Zi - on— our tongues were stilled, our
home-less-ness and ex - ile we on - ly ask for

our tongues were stilled, our
we on - ly ask for

in - stru-ments un-used; how could we sing a ho-ly song of wor - ship
what is sure-ly right: re - mem-ber those whose cruel-ty harmed our child - ren,

mere - ly to keep our con - que - rors a - mused?
and those who glad - ly ri - di - culed our plight.

3. How shall we sing the Lord's song in a strange land? But

if we will not praise, what are we worth? In you we find our

home-land and our hope, Lord;   you are our song,   our great - est   joy   on

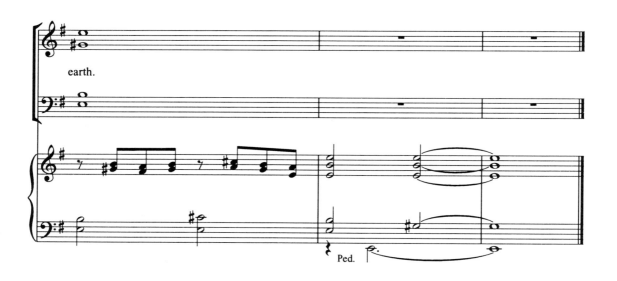

earth.

Ped.

Holy God, I cry for mercy

Psalm 143

Martin E. Leckebusch

Andrew Wright

INGRAVE 87 85

1. Ho - ly God, I cry for mer - cy –
3. An as - sail - ant now pur - sues me,
5. By your love dis - arm my foes, Lord;

not that I de - serve your care, but, since you are al - ways faith - ful,
tries to snatch my hope a - way, till my crushed and faint - ing spi - rit
lead me through this time of strife; gra - cious God, I am your ser - vant,

hear my ur - gent prayer.
trem - bles with dis - may.
now and all my life.

Last time

Harmony

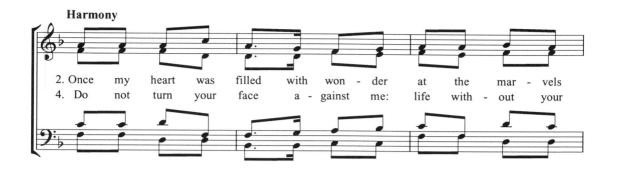

2. Once my heart was filled with won - der at the mar - vels
4. Do not turn your face a - gainst me: life with - out your

you had planned; now my soul is thir - sty for you
love is bleak. Your de - liv - 'rance, guid - ance, ref - uge —

like a de - sert land.
these, my God, I seek.

INDEXES

Index of Psalms for the Common Worship Lectionary

Index of Psalms for the Catholic Lectionary

The Hebrew Psalm numbers have been used in this book, the Catholic (Vulgate) numbers have been added in brackets to this index for ease of reference.

Thematic Index

Index of first lines